Brownie Guide Handbook

Author
Lynda Neilands

Illustrators
Jenny Mumford
Gay Galsworthy ('How To' section)

Designer
Chris McLeod

Price £1.35

Girl Guides Association

© Girl Guides Association 1987
Typeset by Glyn Davies, Cambridge
Printed by W.S. Cowell Ltd, Ipswich

SHOP HOURS

MON. TUES. WED. FRI.   10 am - 3 pm
THURSDAY   10 am - 6 pm
SAT. (Except JULY, AUG.)   9.30 am - 4 pm

'Great! I'm seven! I can be a Brownie now.'

1

'Please can I join the Brownies, Mum?'
she asks her mother at breakfast.

'I'll telephone Mrs James and ask her,'
her Mum replies.

Mrs James said she would love to have
Emily in the Pack.

And so, on Friday afternoon, Emily
dresses, washes her face, pulls on a pair of
bright orange socks and sets off for
Brownies for the very first time.

Everyone looks very busy! Emily wants to join in but it's a bit scary.

Emily's made her Promise.
She is now a proper Brownie with a
uniform and badge to prove it.
She's been joining in all the games
and actitivies.

MAKING THINGS

KEEPING HEALTHY

LENDING A HAND

She's one of the friendliest Brownies in the
Pack . . .

. . . which is why we've asked her to be
your friend right from the beginning and to
help *you* to become a proper Brownie too.

4

'There's so much to tell you about Brownies. I'll start with Brownie Sixes. This is my Six.'

THIS IS MY SIX.

LINDA   SUE   JILL   HELEN   KAREN

'Brownie Packs are made up of Sixes, each with a different name. My Six is called the Pixies. Linda is the leader (called Sixer) and Karen is the Second. Karen helps Linda to run the Six. Sometimes when I don't understand something I ask Linda to explain.'

Baaaa!

Baaa!

Baaaa

Baaaa!

'Sixes work together at meetings. Here we are acting out a nursery rhyme for the rest of the Pack. Can you tell what it is?'

'Here are all the Brownie Six names and Emblems.'

6

'There's a page for writing about your Six in your *Brownie Promise Book*.'

The Brownie Guide Song

The Brownie Guide Ring

'The Guiders make a gate. We skip through in our Sixes singing the Brownie Song to "lah" and clapping.

'We form a circle round the toadstool while we sing the song.

'Then it is time for notices – Mrs James reminds us of dates and times of any special events. She also collects our weekly subscriptions (the money we bring, so that she can pay for all the different things the Pack needs).

'You may form your circle round a Brownie flag, a pool or large World Badge, but you will make it in the same way as we do, and you'll sing the same song. Sometimes, before leaving the Ring, we all hold hands and sing the song again.'

THIS IS THE WAY WE MAKE A BROWNIE RING.

Brownie Bells

The Brownie Guide Salute

'Bring your right hand up to your shoulder, palm out, fingers straight. Now hold your little finger down with your thumb. That's it!'

THIS IS HOW WE SALUTE.

'Brownie Guides, Guides, Ranger Guides, Young Leaders, Guiders and Commissioners all salute in this way. It is a sign that we all belong to the same Guide family and have made a Promise with three parts. (Three parts – three fingers.)'

'Saluting with your right hand means using your left hand to shake hands – unless you've got a spare hand!'

The Brownie Guide Motto ▰▰▰

'"I've only one pair of hands!" Mum used to say when the telephone rang and Sophie cried and Nipper wanted to go out all at the same time.'

waaa-waaaa!

'She can't say *that* now because I'm a Brownie. The Brownie Guide Motto is "Lend a Hand" (L.A.H. for short), so now Mum has a second pair of hands in the house . . . . . MINE!'

'These are my Lend a Hand pictures for last week. (Jill helped me draw them.) As you can see it isn't only Mum who needs a hand. Teachers and neighbours and all sorts of other people do too.'

Miss Pringle

Me

Me

Uncle Bob next door

leaves

buttons

Sophie Me

'So wherever you are, remember our Motto and be ready to carry it out. There's a page for *your* L.A.H. drawings in your *Brownie Promise Book*.'

The Pack Salute

'Here we are welcoming a Brownie who has just made her Promise. We are giving her a Pack Salute.

'We clap three times, once above our heads, once to the right and once to the left. With each clap we call "Welcome". Then we stand still and salute, and our new member salutes back.'

'Sometimes, we can use different words. When Sue's dad showed us a film on road safety, we said "Thank you", instead of "Welcome" each time we clapped.'

'And when Jill won first prize in a colouring competition we said "Well done".'

The Pow-wow Ring

LET'S HOLD A POW-WOW.

A POW-WOW? WHAT'S THAT?

IT'S WHERE WE MAKE PLANS.

THINKING CAPS ON, BROWNIES, WE NEED IDEAS FOR OUR NEXT VENTURE.

'A Venture is a sort of Brownie adventure

'We all thought hard and then Sue put two fingers into the circle – our secret sign showing she wanted to speak.'

'Soon everyone was making suggestions (one at a time, of course), and with some help from our Guiders, we planned something very exciting.'

Later Emily will tell you more about that special Venture. Right now, you have something exciting to do. It's time to make your Brownie Promise.'

The Brownie Guide Promise

A Brownie prepares to make her Promise in three ways: she must hear or read the Brownie Story (so that she knows where the name Brownies came from.)

She must know how to wear her uniform (so that she will look like a proper Brownie).

She must understand the Promise and Law (because keeping the Promise and Law is what Brownies are about).

The next part of your Handbook will help you with these preparations. Start by looking through the Brownie Story which begins on the opposite page. If you can't read very well, don't worry. Just ask someone to read it to you, and you can follow the pictures.

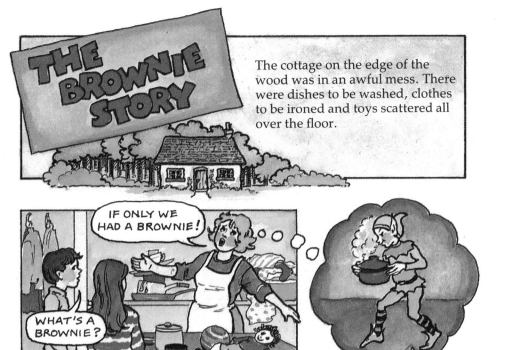

THE BROWNIE STORY

The cottage on the edge of the wood was in an awful mess. There were dishes to be washed, clothes to be ironed and toys scattered all over the floor.

IF ONLY WE HAD A BROWNIE!

WHAT'S A BROWNIE?

Tommy and Betty didn't care. They hated boring old housework.

'What am I to do?' their mother sighed. 'I can't keep the cottage tidy. If only we had a Brownie!'

'What's a Brownie?' asked Tommy.

'A Brownie is a magical little creature, who slips into houses very early before anyone is awake. It tidies toys, irons clothes, washes dishes and does all sorts of helpful things, in secret' replied his mother.

HOW CAN WE GET ONE?

'That's great! How can we get one?' Betty wondered.

THE WISE OWL WOULD KNOW.

'The Wise Owl in the wood would know I suppose,' her mother said.

17

Late that night, Tommy and Betty crept out of the cottage into the wood. It was cold and dark and full of shadows. Or were they ghosts?

'We can't go back. We've got to find the Wise Owl,' said Betty firmly.

'Twitt Twoo. How do you do?' a voice hooted at them from a nearby tree.

'The Wise Owl!' Tommy hugged Betty in relief. And soon the children were seated on a branch, snuggling close to the big bird's feathers.

They explained they were looking for a Brownie.

'Do you know where we could find one?' asked Betty.

'Indeed I doo,' hooted the Owl, and, placing her beak close to Betty's left ear, she explained.

'Tommy, imagine!' exclaimed Betty. 'There's a Brownie in that pool over there. I've got to go to the pool, turn round three times and say:

'Twist me and turn me and show me the elf, I looked in the water and there saw . . .'

'Who? Who? Whoo?' hooted the Owl. 'Look into the water and you'll find your Brownie looking back at you. Her name will finish the rhyme.'

The children raced over to the pool. Betty did exactly as the Owl had said:

'Twist me and turn me and show me the elf, I looked in the water and there saw . . . . .' She looked into the pool.

'Well, can you see it? Can you see a Brownie?' yelled Tommy, hopping from foot to foot in excitement.'

'No,' said Betty. 'All I can see is my reflection.'

Tommy and Betty were so tired and so disappointed that by the time they reached the tree again, they were in tears.

'Boo, hoo hoo. What's the matter with you two?' hooted the Owl, offering them a hanky.

'We didn't find a Brownie,' sniffed Betty. 'I saw no one in the water but myself.'

'Well, well,' said the Owl. 'Let's see if *that* fits the rhyme.'

'Twist me and turn me and show me the elf, I looked in the water and there saw . . . . .'

'Myself!' finished Betty, 'But I'm not a Brownie!'

'Too true, too true,' hooted the Owl. 'But you could act like one for a change and so could Tommy. It would be fun.'

Tommy and Betty returned thoughtfully to the cottage. If you had passed that way very early next morning, you would have seen a lamp burning in the kitchen window and two figures busily scurrying about inside.

And when the children's mother came down for breakfast, she couldn't believe her eyes. There wasn't a toy in sight. Everything was clean and tidy.

'Why a Brownie has been here. How wonderful!' she gasped.

From that day to this, the cottage has been like a different place. And Tommy and Betty have been like different children. They never get bored now; they are so busy planning their secret Good Turns.

Of course, their mother has discovered the truth. She thinks she is very lucky to have such helpful children. And Tommy and Betty have discovered how right the Wise Owl was: being human Brownies is FUN!

BEING A BROWNIE IS FUN!

THE END

Now that you have read The Brownie Story you will understand:

– where the name 'Brownie' came from,

– why some Brownie Guiders are called Brown Owl,

– why some Brownie Packs place a pool at the centre of their Ring.

You may also be interested to know:

– that make-believe Brownies were supposed to dance round toadstools, which is why some Packs have a toadstool at the centre of the ring.

21

How to Wear your Uniform

Linda is showing you how to wear your uniform properly.

'If you want your tie to look fresh and clean, don't forget to wash it.'

THIS IS THE PROMISE BADGE. YOU WEAR IT ON THE CROSS-OVER PART OF YOUR TIE.

'Your pockets will hold small things that might otherwise disappear – like your pencil and your money.

'Sometimes your belt will need a special rub to keep it shiny.

'If you feel cold in winter, wear a brown cardigan over your uniform.'

'Dont forget to wear your hat to meetings. And make sure your name is inside – in case you lose it.'

'The tape with the name of your Pack should be sewn on your left shoulder seam. Below it some Brownies sew a badge showing in which country or county they are a Brownie.'

'Your Six Emblem is worn on the left, below the end of your tie.'

'Wear brown or black shoes, if possible; and as clean as you can make them!

'Socks should be white, dark brown or fawn (not orange!) You can wear fawn or brown tights, or brown trousers in winter.

'Uniforms help us to really *feel* like Brownies. That's why you wear yours for the first time the day you make your Promise.'

The Brownie Guide Promise

Here is an example of a Promise:

Emily wanted one of her Six to wait for her after Brownies.
Helen said, 'I might wait.'
And Karen said, 'I'll probably wait.'
But it wasn't until Sue said, 'I promise I'll wait,' that Emily was content.
Why? Because Sue had used those two important words 'I promise'; so Emily knew she would be there.

When we promise something we are telling people that we really mean to do what we say.

Once you understand how important a promise is, you are ready to look at the special Promise made by Brownie Guides. Brownies all over the world make a Promise like this.

THE BROWNIE GUIDE PROMISE

I promise that I will do my best:
To do my duty to God,
To serve the Queen
and help other people
and
To keep the Brownie Guide Law.

Do you remember why Brownies salute with three fingers? It's because the Promise has three parts.

A Brownie needs to know not only the words of her Promise, but also what each part means; she does not want to be like the girl who was asked to bring her brother's favourite comic back from town.

'I promise I will', she said.

But when she reached the shop and saw all the different comics, she felt silly. She'd forgotten to find out the name of his favourite, so she didn't know which one to buy.

Promising something, without thinking about it first, can lead to problems.

That's why every sensible Brownie spends some time thinking about each part of her Promise before she makes it.

Let's think about the first part now:

I promise that I will do my best:
To do my duty to God.

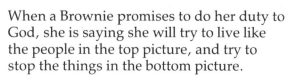

When a Brownie promises to do her duty to God, she is saying she will try to live like the people in the top picture, and try to stop the things in the bottom picture.

How else can Brownies do their duty to God?

Here are some Brownies
keeping the first part of their
Promise.

'I talk or pray to God about the
things which happen to me each
day.'

'I say sorry to God when I've
done something wrong.'

'I give thanks for everything I
have been given – my home, my
food, my family and my
friends.'

'I try to learn more about God
week by week.'

Your Promise goes on
to underline something
God asks every Brownie
to do, which is . . .

To serve the Queen and help other people.

'I can't serve the Queen. I don't live anywhere near Buckingham Palace,' a new Brownie was once heard to wail, and she was happy to find that serving the Queen didn't mean washing Palace windows or vacuuming Palace carpets.

She could keep the second part of her Promise without leaving her home town.

CAN YOU THINK HOW?

The answer is quite simple really. Our Queen works hard to make our country and all the countries of which she is Queen or Head happy places for people to live. Serving the Queen means helping her with this work. It means looking round your area to see what needs to be done. Is there litter in the park? Are there old people who feel lonely?

If you were to ask these Brownies what they were doing, they might say. 'We're visiting our friends in Riverside House,' and that answer would be right. But they could also say 'We're serving the Queen,' and that answer would be right too.

When Brownies help other people they serve the Queen at the same time.

29

The Brownie Guide Law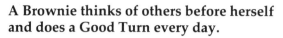

A Brownie thinks of others before herself and does a Good Turn every day.

In the third part of the Promise, Brownies promise to keep this Law. Usually this means trying to keep it in their own home.

Sometimes keeping the Law is easy.

Good Turns can be fun!

Sometimes it is very difficult.

But remember how much unexpected happiness Tommy and Betty found when they stopped being selfish.

KEEPING THE BROWNIE GUIDE LAW IS **ALWAYS** WORTH IT IN THE END !

The Brownie Promise Ceremony

This is what happened at Emily's Promise Ceremony.

The Pack formed a circle round the Brownie toadstool.
Linda, Emily's Sixer, took her by the hand and
together they skipped into the centre where her
Guider, Mrs James, was waiting.

Emily stood facing her Guider.

'Do you know the Brownie
Guide Law?'

'A Brownie thinks of others
before herself and does a Good
Turn every day.'

'Do you know that if you make
the Promise, you must always
do your best to keep it, and
carry it out everywhere, but
especially at home?' asked
Mrs James.

'Yes,' replied Emily.

'Will you make your Promise as
a Brownie Guide?'

After this final question Emily
repeated her Promise, saluting
as she spoke, and the rest of
the Pack saluted too.

31

'I promise that I will do my best:
to do my duty to God,
to serve the Queen and help
other people and to keep the
Brownie Guide Law,' said
Emily.

'I trust you to keep the Promise!'
replied Mrs James.

Then the whole Pack gave Emily a Pack
Salute, and Emily felt hot, relieved and
very pleased with herself all at once.

I'M A **REAL** BROWNIE NOW!

If you have been coming to Brownies for
four weeks or more, and if your Guider
agrees that you have done everything we
talked about on page 16 of your Handbook
then you are ready to make your Promise
too.

Your Pack will be looking forward to
welcoming you.

The way they do it may be slightly different
to the way Emily's Pack welcomed her, but
the Promise Ceremony will be exactly the
same.

To make everything
clear the words you
will speak during the
Ceremony have been
printed in blue and
the words your
Guider will say are
printed in red.

32

The Brownie Guide Badge

Here is a close-up view of the Badge you will receive.

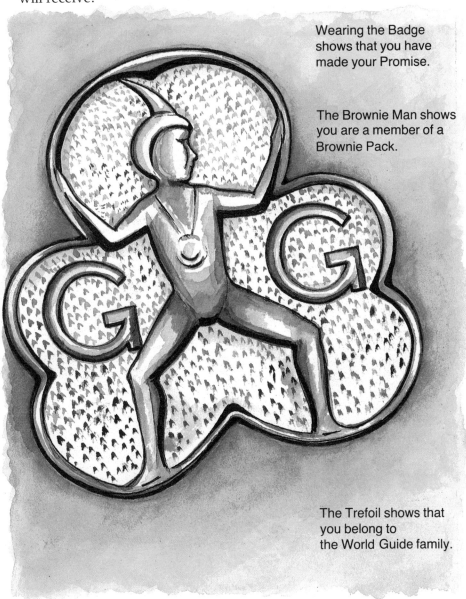

Wearing the Badge shows that you have made your Promise.

The Brownie Man shows you are a member of a Brownie Pack.

The Trefoil shows that you belong to the World Guide family.

The World Badge

Did you know that in almost every country in the world you have Brownie sisters (millions of them!). Guides and Brownies everywhere wear a World Badge, which looks like this:

A Brownie Prayer

Because your Promise is so important it is a
good idea to ask God to help you keep it.

Brownies in many Packs use the words of
this Prayer:

Dear Father in Heaven
We know we are your children
We want to serve you faithfully;
We want to keep our Brownie Guide Promise.
Help us to listen to your voice;
Help us to be willing
and quick to do your work;
Help us to be friendly and loving;
and help us to thank you every day
For all your gifts to us.
Amen.

Any Questions?

On the following pages are answers to questions new Brownies often ask:

Question

'How did Brownies begin?'

Answer

Over seventy years ago a man called Lord Baden-Powell had the wonderful idea which started Scouts and Guides. Many of the girls coming to Guides had small sisters who saw all the interesting and exciting things Guides did. They wanted to join in, so it was decided to start a group for them called the Rosebuds. But soon it became clear that although the Rosebuds loved their meetings, they didn't like their name. People tried to think of a better one, and in the end Lord Baden-Powell remembered a story he had heard about certain helpful mischievous creatures . . . and as you've probably guessed, the Rosebuds have been Brownies ever since.

To begin with, the Rosebuds wore blue uniforms like the Guides, but later the colour of their uniform changed to match their name.

Question

'Our Guider said February 22nd was a sort of Guiding Birthday. What did she mean?'

Answer

February 22nd is the birthday both of Lord Baden-Powell, the Founder of our Movement, and of Lady Olave Baden-Powell, his wife, who was the World Chief Guide. On this date every year, Brownies, Guides and Rangers all over the world have a day of celebration called Thinking Day.

On Thinking Day, everyone thinks about the World Guide Family. Often there are services and special Thinking Day meetings at which Brownies pray for their sisters around the world and give money to help them, through the Thinking Day Fund.

They have a lot of fun too. Here are members of Emily's Pack dressed for a Thinking Day party. Can you find out which countries they represent?

Question

'What happens to the money collected each week at Brownie Meetings?'

Answer

Every Brownie Pack has expenses. Money is needed to buy badges, books and equipment. It is also needed for Good Turns and Ventures – to hire a bus, for example, or to buy biscuits for a Parents' Evening. The Brownie Hall can be another expense; many Packs make a contribution each year to the cost of heat and light. And every Pack sends money each year to Commonwealth Headquarters to help keep the whole Guide Association running smoothly.

So you can see how important it is to remember your subscription. With all these expenses, every penny counts.

Brownie Activities

'Now that you're a real Brownie, I'm going to tell you about the special things Brownies do.'

BROWNIE FOOTPATH

BROWNIE JOURNEYS AND CHALLENGES

INTEREST BADGES

PACK VENTURES

BROWNIE PANTO
Hammington
School Hall
Saturday in 11.03
Admission 20p

'As you can see from these pictures, Brownies sometimes work on their own, but very often the whole Pack will plan an activity and carry it out together. We call that a Pack Venture.'

'But whatever the Venture, we must remember that each of us, from the smallest to the tallest, is needed.'

'There'll be a special part for YOU in your Pack Ventures. Can you think of something you are good at? Something you enjoy doing?

'In my Six . . .

Linda always has lots of ideas.
Karen can sew and knit and write very neatly.
Jill is good at drawing and painting.
Helen runs like the wind and knows how to ride.
Sue is always smiling and friendly. She's really good at tidying up.
EVERYONE is good at something.

'So when we go on Ventures we work together with all the other Brownies in our Pack to make the Venture a success.'

The Story of our Latest Venture ∎

'Look back to page 15. Our Venture began in the Pow-wow Ring. Sue told us about an Indian village she had seen on T.V. "The women who live there have to walk miles each day to fetch water," she said. "They really need their own well. Could we lend a hand to make one?" "We could send money" suggested Kate. "But how can we get it?"

There were lots of ideas, then Linda asked, "What about a pet show? We could enter our pets and invite Brownies from the other side of town!"

This is the invitation we sent. Jill designed it.'

WHAT ABOUT A PET SHOW?

WE COULD SEND MONEY.

2nd Hammington BROWNIE PACK Invites you to a PET SHOW for India

Saturday 2nd April
3.30 pm
Hammington School Playground
Admission 50p

THE FOLLOWING WEEK

'The next week, we made lots of rosettes as prizes out of red, blue and yellow tissue paper.'

1st PRIZE

'We asked Mr Barnes, the vet, to act as judge.'

I'LL BE DELIGHTED TO BE THE JUDGE.

THE NEXT SATURDAY

'On the day, the school playground was full of animals – dogs, cats, rabbits, goldfish . . . . . Kate even brought her pony and gave rides.'

'Any Brownies without pets had the job of announcing the classes.
By five o'clock the judging was over and the Sixers were able to count the money. "We've almost fifty pounds to send to the Fund," Linda shrieked.'

A FEW WEEKS LATER

'A few weeks later we got a letter from the Fund organiser. "Drilling has begun and soon the village will have its new well", said Mrs James.
We all cheered. What a great Venture!'

HOORAY!!!

'Remembering special Ventures is fun.
'Actually some of the Ventures I showed
you on page 40 happened before I joined
our Pack. I heard about them from Linda.
Why not ask your Guider or one of the
older Brownies to tell you what your Pack
has done.'

The Venture Badge

'Have you seen anyone with a badge like
this on their uniform? It's called a Venture
Badge and shows that the wearer has done
her best in a Pack Venture.

'After our Pet Show every Brownie in the
Pack was wearing one. We hadn't all done
the same things. It was Linda who had the
idea, and Jill who designed the invitation;
but we all helped make rosettes and even
more important, we all turned up on the
day. And afterwards, when the visitors had
left, we all stayed behind to tidy up.'

'Right now our Pack isn't on a Venture, but that doesn't mean I've nothing to do.

'I want to become a really experienced Brownie, able to carry out my Promise in bigger, more adventurous ways.'

'I want to be a really good Brownie, to try new things and practise them.'

'In-between-Venture times, are times for learning, discovering and practising.'

'This is where Brownie Journeys and Interest Badges come in.'

45

Interest Badges

'Here is a Brownie Interest Badge.'

'Can you guess what it is given for? Yes, for good drawings and paintings. It's the Artist Badge.

'There are about thirty of these triangular badges altogether, each awarded for a different interest and with a different picture in the centre. The *Brownie Guide Badge Book* explains all about them, and the booklets about the different badges will help you.'

'When you have made your Promise you can work for any Interest Badge you want.'

'After Jill designed the invitations for our Pet Show, she thought she would like to work for her Artist's Badge. She asked Mrs James about it (you should always ask your Guider before beginning a badge), and together they looked it up in the *Brownie Guide Badge Book* to see what she had to do.'

'For the next few weeks, Jill was very busy drawing and colouring in her spare time. Then, when the work was finished, Mrs James arranged for her test.

'The tester was an art student called Dave. He admired Jill's uniform (it's important to wear your uniform, for a test), and said her drawings were "very promising". He showed her how to draw a hippopotamus.

'Of course, she passed the test, and was given an Artist's Badge to sew onto the right sleeve of her uniform.'

'Linda's first Interest Badge was the Swimmer's Badge. She did it as one of the Journey Challenges, I'll be telling you about it in a moment.'

'Next, with lots of other Brownies, she worked for her Jester Badge, as part of a Pack Venture.'

'Now she has MILLIONS of badges!

'But Mrs James says, "The best Brownie is the Brownie who tries hardest to keep her Promise, not the one with the most badges, and the best reason for doing an Interest Badge is to learn a new way of helping others."'

WELL OVER TEN ANYWAY!

Brownie Journeys and Challenges

'Every year, we spend in Brownies we make an imaginary journey;

Brownies who are seven travel along a Footpath.'

'Brownies who are eight travel along a Road.'

AS WE TRAVEL WE MEET CHALLENGES.

'Brownies who are nine travel along a Highway.'

'As we travel, we meet Challenges. These are new things to learn and do, which help us to become really expert Brownies.

'There are eight different kinds of Challenge, so we work for eight Challenges on each journey.'

What is a Challenge?

'If I can do something without any effort . . .'

'. . . then it ISN'T a real Challenge.'

'A real Challenge isn't easy.'

'It means practising and doing my very best. That's the way to improve.'

Brownie Footpath

Here are Brownies journeying along the Brownie Footpath, working on eight different Challenges.

It doesn't matter which Challenge they do first. A Brownie on a Brownie Journey decides with her Guider.

Are YOU ready to travel with Emily along the Brownie Footpath?

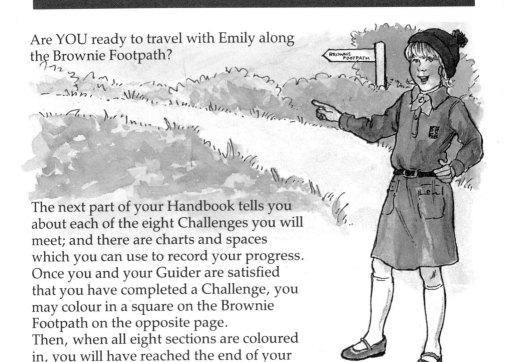

The next part of your Handbook tells you about each of the eight Challenges you will meet; and there are charts and spaces which you can use to record your progress. Once you and your Guider are satisfied that you have completed a Challenge, you may colour in a square on the Brownie Footpath on the opposite page.
Then, when all eight sections are coloured in, you will have reached the end of your Journey, and will receive your Brownie Footpath Badge.

You will find hints on how to go about some of the Challenges at the back of your Handbook.

And if you see Freda the Elephant in the corner of a page, she is there to remind you of your Promise.

DON'T FORGET!

Always remember to put other people first and try to turn Challenges into Good Turns.

My Progress Along the Brownie Footpath

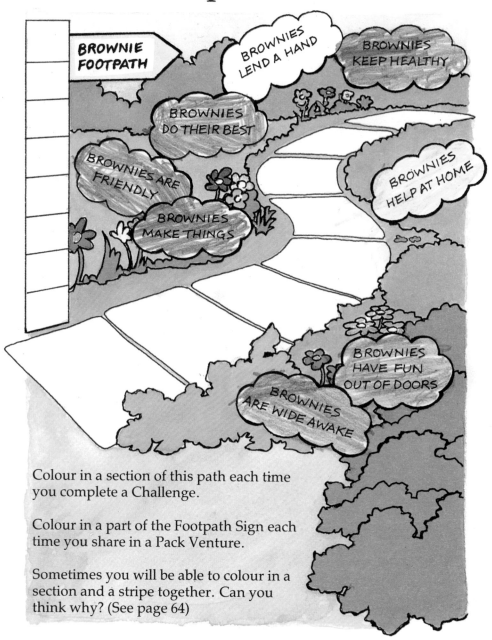

BROWNIE FOOTPATH

BROWNIES LEND A HAND

BROWNIES KEEP HEALTHY

BROWNIES DO THEIR BEST

BROWNIES ARE FRIENDLY

BROWNIES MAKE THINGS

BROWNIES HELP AT HOME

BROWNIES HAVE FUN OUT OF DOORS

BROWNIES ARE WIDE AWAKE

Colour in a section of this path each time you complete a Challenge.

Colour in a part of the Footpath Sign each time you share in a Pack Venture.

Sometimes you will be able to colour in a section and a stripe together. Can you think why? (See page 64)

Brownies are Wide Awake

It's good to be Wide Awake! If you walk
around in a daydream you will miss all
kinds of interesting and important things.

Choose at least one of the four Wide Awake
Challenges on these pages and carry it out;
or, if you prefer, you may think up a new
Wide Awake Challenge of your own.

Go for an 'I Spy' walk looking for different
kinds of birds, flowers, chimney pots, T.V.
aerials, signs of the seasons or anything
else of interest.

On my 'I Spy' walk I went

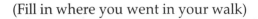

(Fill in where you went in your walk)

I saw

(In this box, draw a picture of all the
different things you saw and label them.)

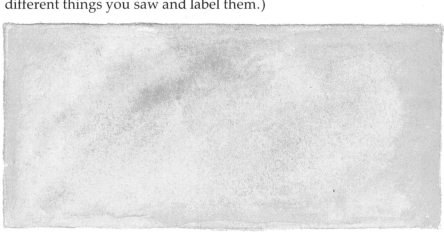

Do you recognise any of these badges and Emblems? Find out what they are called from the Brownies you see wearing them, and fill in the names beside each picture.

GIRL GUIDES

Animal Lover

GIRL GUIDES

GIRL GUIDES

descoverey

Path finder

HIGHWAY
GIRL GUIDES

birthday badge

sixer badge

high way

Gnome

Kelpie

Be Wide Awake at home. Carry out this Indoor Safety Challenge.

SPOT THE GOOD TURNS
IN THE PICTURE

What can Rachel and her brother do to stop accidents in their home?

Your eyes, ears, hands and nose can tell you a lot if your brain is paying attention.

Take part in a game using your senses, (touching, listening, looking or smelling).

The Wide Awake game I played was called:

negty   game

In it I used my eyes,   ears,   hands,   nose

Put a line under your answer.

Or complete your Wide Awake Challenge
in some other way.

Every Sunday, Emily travels by bus to visit
her Granny. She has discovered a way of
keeping Wide Awake on the journey. She
counts animals. The first time she did this
she saw three hens, six dogs, two cats,
eleven fields full of cows, four fields full of
sheep, and a rabbit. Afterwards she drew
pictures of them, and Mrs James agreed
that she had completed her Wide Awake
Challenge.

If you have completed your Wide Awake
Challenge in a special way, write about it,
or draw a picture of it on this page.

MY WIDE AWAKE CHALLENGE

Brownies Keep Healthy

Your body is a machine. Keep it working well, inside and out.

Emily saw this picture in the doctor's waiting room.

'Yuck! Is that what I look like inside!' she said.

Then the doctor told her the names of some different parts of the body and explained what each part did.

Here is an enlargement of the picture. See if you can label each part correctly from the list of names on the right-hand side of the page.

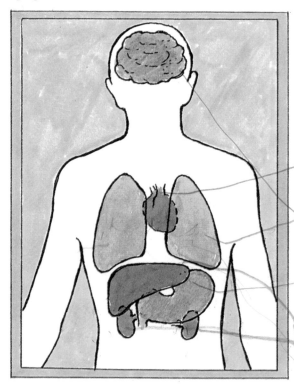

HEART

LUNGS

BRAIN

STOMACH

KIDNEYS

LIVER

Now match the parts of the body with the jobs they do.
(Emily has done the first one for you.)

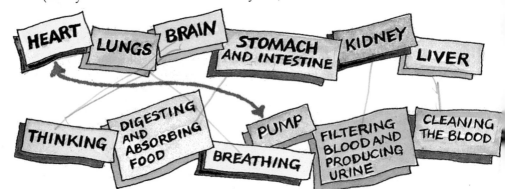

One way of looking after your body is by taking exercise.

Do *one* of the following:

a) Throw a bean bag to land four times out of six in a box, positioned as far away from you as possible. (See page 117.)

b) Learn to skip backwards. (See page 117.)

c) See how many times you can bounce a ball without a break. Challenge yourself to improve. (See page 117.)

d) Jump the Blob. (See page 118.)

OR Challenge yourself with any other way of keeping yourself fit and healthy.

Write about what you have done in the space below.

My Keeping Healthy Challenge was bouncing ball and skipping

Looking after yourself outside means
taking care of your appearance.

These are some of the things you can use.

Make a special effort to look after either
your nails or your teeth or your hair this
week. (See page 118-119.)

In the box draw either a nail-brush, a
toothbrush or a hair brush, each with seven
tufts. Colour in one tuft each day you carry
out your Challenge.

KEEP IT UP!

This week I am taking special care of my

_____

Brownies Do their Best

If you know there is a prize for doing something you will probably do your best to win it; but doing your best without any prize is a real Challenge.

For a week do your best in *two* of the following:

a) Smile every time you want to grumble or are hurt.

b) Eat your food without complaining.

c) Thank God for something every day.

d) Go to bed when you are told.

e) Do a job you don't like.

f) Be kind to someone who is sick.

OR Do your best in some other way you don't find easy.

Here are two cakes, each with seven candles. Draw a light on top of a candle each time you do your best this week.

DO YOUR BEST!

Brownies Make Things

Brownies can make toys and decorations with their hands, and they can make stories and poems in their heads. They can make a story come to life by acting or miming it.

At a Brownie meeting make *one* of the following:

a) A greetings card.

b) A decoration, e.g. for Christmas or New Year. (See page 120.)

c) A toy. (See page 121.)

d) A model.

e) Help your Six to make up a poem or mime.

OR Make anything else you choose.

For my Making Things Challenge I made

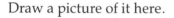
ballanda   Prayr Book

Draw a picture of it here.

Put a tick in this box if you tidied up afterwards.

The Challenge that Grew ▰

For her Footpath Challenge Karen made a
Christmas decoration. It was so pretty that
other Brownies wanted to make one too.

> IT'S LOVELY!

> I'D LIKE TO
> TRY THAT.

> HOW DID YOU
> DO IT?

'Could we have a Christmas decoration-
making Venture?' Emily asked.

'That's a good idea!' Mrs James agreed.

'We could take some decorations round to
the old people's flats where my granny and
grandpa live,' said Linda.

'And sing carols for them,' added Sue.

Challenges grow into Ventures as
easily as that.

And during a Venture Brownies often find
themselves completing a Challenge.

Brownies are Friendly

Brownies start by being friendly with the members of their own Six and go on to discover Brownie friends all over the world.

Help your Six with at least *two* Six activities.

You could make something together, play a game or do a job together, or of course, work together on a Venture.

Draw pictures and write in these boxes to show what you have done.

Brownie friends need to find out about each other.

Do *one* of the following:

a) Play a Brownie game or sing a Brownie song from another country.

b) Hear, tell or read a story from another country in which there are Brownies.

c) Find out what is special about February 22nd.

OR Work out another Challenge with your Guider.

BEING FRIENDLY IS FUN!

FREDA

Here are some Brownies from other parts of the world. They have lost the names of their countries.

Match each Brownie with her country and write in the name on her banner.

INDONESIA

PANAMA SPAIN

AUSTRALIA NIGERIA

SWEDEN INDIA

Brownies Lend a Hand

Make Freda a happy elephant.

Here's how:

Remember to do a different Good Turn every day for one week and draw or write about it in the Elephant House.

MAKE ME HAPPY!

SUNDAY
laid the table

MONDAY
Wash the dishes

THURSDAY
dry the dishes

TUESDAY
Went shoping

FRIDAY
Dusted

WEDNESDAY
Wash the table

SATURDAY
hovered

Also challenge yourself to Lend a Hand in a special way by doing *one* of the following:

a) Take part in a Good Turn Venture ☐
with your Pack.

b) Do a special job for your Guider. ☐

c) Make, wash or mend some Pack ☐
equipment. (See page 122.)

OR Make up your own Lend a Hand ☐
Challenge.

Put a tick in the box opposite the Challenge you choose.

Brownies Help at Home ▬

There are lots of opportunities to be helpful at home.

Choose and do *two* of the following:

a) Help with washing up or laying a table. (See page 123.)

b) Clean shoes or muddy boots. (See page 124.)

c) Clean out a bath or shower.

d) Make sandwiches.

OR Do some other helpful job.

These are some of the materials you need to help at home. Tick the ones you used in carrying out your Challenge.

KEEP BUSY!

Brownies Have Fun Out-of-Doors

There are wonderful things to discover and enjoy in nature.

Do *one* of the following:

a) Using natural materials make a gift. (See page 129)

b) Name five birds, or five flowers, or five trees which you have seen and find out something about them.

c) Make a weather chart. (See page 125)

OR Enjoy yourself out-of-doors in some other way.

Write about what you did (or draw a picture of it) in this space.

This is what Karen wrote about her Out-of-Doors Challenge.

I went to the beach. I gathered a lot of shells. I stuck the smallest prettiest shells onto a matchbox. I gave the box to my Mum as a present.

Now you have reached the end of the
Brownie Footpath.

And look who's here!

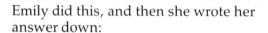

HI THERE!

Freda is always very keen to meet Brownies
at the end of a Journey.
She likes them to look back over what they
have learned and to think how they have
kept their Promise.

Emily did this, and then she wrote her
answer down:

How I kept my Promise by Emily.
This Journey helped me to keep my Promise better.
I go to bed now when I'm told even if I want to
watch T.V. This is doing my best. It gives me
time to say thank you to God.
On this Journey I washed dishes and tidied the
Brownie cupboard and did not fight with Sophie
in the bus because I was Wide Awake counting
animals. This is helping other people, especially
My Mum.

WELL DONE
EMILY!

You may not feel able to put your answer
on paper, but Freda will be quite happy if
you chat it over with your Guider.

Once you have done this, you will receive
your Brownie Footpath Badge.

The Brownie Birthday Badge

It's exactly one year since Emily made her Brownie Promise. Today, at the meeting, she celebrated her Brownie Birthday. Of course, she didn't get presents like she did for her ordinary birthday last month, but it was still a special occasion. Mrs James presented her with her first Brownie Birthday Badge, Linda gave her a card from her Six (it had a copy of the Promise inside) and the whole Pack gave her a Pack Salute.

'It's like having my Promise Ceremony all over again,' Emily said.

For every year you spend as a Brownie, like Emily, you will receive a Birthday Badge. The first Birthday Badge is brown, the second is green and the third, red.

A Brownie wears her Birthday Badge on the left shoulder of her uniform, and when she gets a new one, she takes the old one off.

71

Position of Badges

Emily hasn't only gained her Footpath Badge and her Brownie Birthday Badge recently, she has also been working for her Animal Lover Badge. Have you started working for *your* first Interest Badge yet?

Here is a close-up view of a Brownie in uniform, showing where the different badges go.

PROMISE BADGE

FOOTPATH BADGE
ROAD BADGE
HIGHWAY BADGE

BROWNIE BIRTHDAY BADGE

PACK NAME TAPE

VENTURE BADGE

COUNTY OR COUNTRY BADGE

INTEREST BADGES (IN PAIRS)

WORLD BADGE

SIX EMBLEM

SIXER/SECOND STRIPE

Brownie Revels

LOOK!

ROBIN HOOD INVITES ALL THE BROWNIES OF THE DISTRICT TO A PARTY WITH MAID MARIAN AND HIS MERRY MEN AT HAMMINGTON FOREST PARK ON SATURDAY 28th MAY AT 3.00 PM

'This is the invitation our Guider read out in our last Pow-wow. I couldn't believe it. *Robin Hood* inviting *me* to a party!

'Then Mrs James explained that our Pack had been invited to Brownie Revels. Lots of other Packs had been invited too, because that's what Brownie Revels are all about. They give Brownies from different Packs a chance to do something together. You never quite know what that something will be.

'On the Saturday of our Revels, Hammington Forest became Sherwood Forest for three hours. The Guiders dressed up. (Can you spot Mrs James?) We had an opening ceremony, played lots of games and finished with a banquet of crisps and orange juice in the Sheriff of Nottingham's Castle.'

Ideas for Ventures

'I wonder what *your* first Brownie Revels will be like? One thing is sure – you will be having fun with Brownies you have never met before. So don't just talk to members of your own Pack. Brownie Revels are a great way of making friends!

'I asked three Brownies I met at our Brownie Revels to tell me their latest Ventures. This is what they said:

My Pack held Spring Sports. We moved round different activities in our Sixes. We found out who was the champion in each activity and we all got points for doing our best.

My Pack had a Friendship Venture. We filled a scrapbook with information about ourselves. We sent it to a Brownie Pack in Canada. Now we're looking forward to getting a scrapbook back from them.

Our last Venture was a visit to the Fire Station. We saw inside a fire-engine. A fireman talked to us about safety in the home and taught us how to make an emergency phone-call.

Your Second Brownie Journey

On page 77 you will find a map of your second Brownie Journey – the journey you make when you are eight. It is along a road this time. As you travel you will meet eight Challenges. Just as a road tends to be bigger than a Footpath, so these Challenges will be bigger than the ones you did last year.

Once you and your Guider agree that you have completed them all, you will receive your Brownie Road Badge.

Of course, you won't be making the Journey alone. Guiders are always there to give help and advice, and you will find hints on certain Challenges at the back of your Handbook. Probably you will be able to carry out some Challenges with other Brownies as part of a Pack Venture.

DON'T FORGET ABOUT ME !

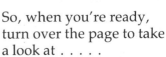

You wouldn't, would you? As you make the Journey, you'll remember your Promise.

So, when you're ready, turn over the page to take a look at . . . . .

My Progress Along the Brownie Road

Each time that you and your Guider agree that you have completed a Challenge, colour in a strip and write in the name of the Challenge on the Brownie Road.

Each time you share in a Pack Venture write what you did on a brick in the Venture Bridge and colour it in.

Draw pictures of Interest Badges you gain on your Journey.

You don't *have* to get six!!

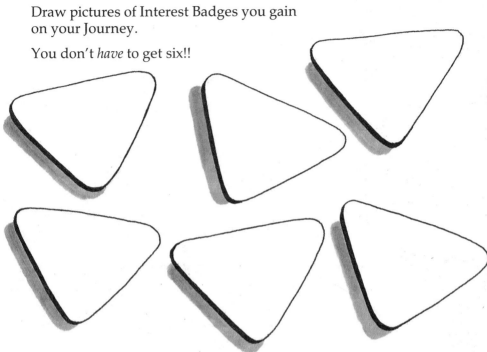

The Brownie Magazine

You will find lots of ideas for Interest Badges, Journey Challenges and Ventures in your own magazine – *The Brownie*.

Emily, Karen and Sue get copies every week and pass them on to the other members of their Six.

Emily likes the stories best (especially when they're about animals), Sue enjoys the puzzles and Karen loves to try out the ideas for making things. What do *you* like best about *The Brownie*? If you don't buy it yourself, why not borrow a copy from a friend or your Guider?

Brownies are Wide Awake

On the Brownie Footpath you learnt to notice what was going on around you. Now you can practise remembering things as well. Do at least *one* of the following:

a) Use a private telephone or a public call box and pass on a message correctly. Know how to contact the Emergency Services. (See page 127.)

b) Remember a shopping list of at least four items. Ask for each item politely.

c) Pass an eye and memory test e.g. Kim's Game.

OR Challenge yourself to notice and remember in some other way.

During this Challenge Emily stored a shopping-list in her memory. Draw a picture of your own head in the space beside Emily's, and draw some things you remembered for your Challenge inside the 'thinks' balloon.

Brownies Keep Healthy

Some foods are better for us than others.
Sometimes we don't eat enough of these.

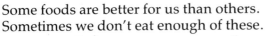

Some foods don't do our bodies much good
and often we eat too much of them.

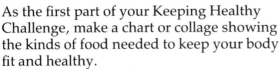

As the first part of your Keeping Healthy
Challenge, make a chart or collage showing
the kinds of food needed to keep your body
fit and healthy.

I completed my Healthy Eating Chart/

Collage on _____
              (fill in the date)

The second part of your Keeping Healthy Challenge involves exercise. Do *one* of the following:

a) Hit a target with a ball or a bean bag from as far away as possible.

b) Do some form of balancing, or show you can bowl a ball between two skittles.

c) Improve on a Challenge you have done already using a ball, a rope or a bean bag.

OR Think up an Exercise Challenge to do yourself.

My Keeping Healthy Exercise ■

Write what you did, inside the beanbag.

As you know Helen is very athletic. For her
Keeping Healthy Exercise Challenge she
decided to work for her Agility Badge.
She found the booklet that Mrs James lent
her very helpful, and passed her test with
flying colours.

Brownies Do their Best

Doing your best is always a Challenge and always worthwhile. For a week try to do your best by doing *two* of the following:

a) Make and keep a Mind Your Tongue Challenge. (See page 128.)

b) Do what you are told quickly, i.e. the first time.

c) Think of others in a special way by praying for different people.

d) Be kind to someone in the Pack who is not your best friend.

e) Do a job you don't like doing.

OR Do your best in some other way.

Draw two flowers each with seven petals and colour one petal each time you carry out your Challenge.

Emily Does her Best

When Emily was on the Brownie Footpath she did her best by going to bed when she was told. Once she was in bed she thanked God for the things that had happened that day.

As her Brownie Road Challenge, she decided to pray for different people. She prayed for her mum, dad, granny, Sophie, Uncle Jim and Auntie Ann; and then wondered who else she could pray for. She remembered Sunita, the new girl, who had just arrived in her class, 'I'll pray that Sunita will be happy in our school' she thought.

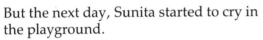

But the next day, Sunita started to cry in the playground.

'Oh, dear' sighed Emily, 'perhaps it would help if I was especially kind to her .

Before long Sunita was smiling. She'd been a Brownie in her last town, Emily discovered, and she was looking forward to joining Emily's Pack . . . especially now she had a friend.

Emily got into bed that night with a warm feeling inside. She'd done her best.

'Thank you, God, that Sunita is happy now, and thank you for giving me a new friend.'

Brownies Make Things

Brownies on the Brownie Road try to make something they haven't already made on the Footpath.

Do *one or more* of the following:

a) Listen to a favourite piece of music and talk to your Guider about it.

b) Try a new craft, e.g. knitting, sewing, crocheting. (See page 130-31.)

c) Make a small flower arrangement for a table from fresh, dried or artificial flowers.

d) Make a picture using a variety of material, e.g. natural materials such as leaves or flowers, cloth, felt or wool.

OR Make something else of your own choice. (Remember you can make something up in your head – a story, poem or even a tune.)

Write about what you have made inside the scroll:

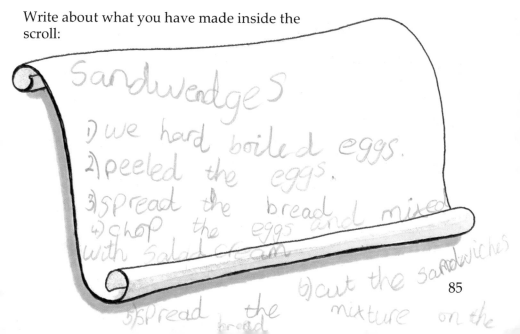

Sandwedges
1) we hard boiled eggs.
2) peeled the eggs.
3) spread the bread and mixed
4) chop the eggs and
with salad cream

5) spread the bread
b) cut the sandwiches
mixture on the

85

Brownies are Friendly

Being friendly means being interested in other people; in meeting them and in finding out about them.

Do *one* of the following:

a) Take part in a Venture in which you meet other people who are not in your Pack.

b) With your Guider's help find out about other people's work in the community, e.g. a clergyman, a policeman, a nurse, a school cleaner, a dustman.

c) Choose one country where there are Brownies, find out all you can about it and point to this country on a map.

OR Show friendliness to others in some other way.

Sue went to the Brownie Revels in Hammington Forest Park. For her Brownie Road Challenge she wrote down some things she discovered about the Brownies she met.

My Discoveries about Others
I met a lot of Brownies from different Packs. I met a Brownie called Sarah and a Brownie called Parveen. Their Pack meets on a Thursday evening and Sarah is a second. She has four interest badges. Parveen has a friendship badge she said Brownies in Bangladesh are called yellowbirds. Her family came from Bangladesh, but she was born in this country.

My Discoveries About Others

Write something you have learnt about others in this box.

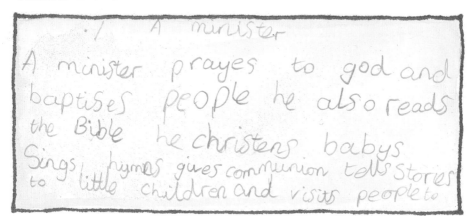

A minister

A minister prayes to god and baptises people he also reads the Bible he christens babys Sings hymns gives communion tells stories to little children and visits people to

Brownies Lend a Hand

Now you are on the Brownie Road you are trusted to act sensibly. The more sensible (or responsible) you are, the better you will be able to Lend a Hand.

Remember to do a Good Turn every day and do *one* of the following:

a) Do a Good Turn for someone where you live or where the Pack meets.

b) Find as many ways as you can of keeping your home safe. (See page 134.)

c) Know the rules of the road and show you know how to keep them (The Green Cross Code).

OR Lend a Hand by acting sensibly and helpfully in some other way. (Perhaps as part of a Pack Venture.)

DO A GOOD TURN EVERY DAY!

Record what you have done by adding a drawing of yourself to this picture; either in the house, on the pavement or amongst people (depending on where you carried out your Challenge).

For my Lend a Hand Challenge I _____

The Green Cross Code

1 First find a safe place to cross, then stop.

2 Stand on the pavement near the kerb.

3 Look all round for traffic and listen.

4 If traffic is coming, let it pass. Look all round again.

5 When there is no traffic near, walk straight across the road.

6 Keep looking and listening for traffic while you cross.

Brownies Help at Home

In your home can you look after something or someone by yourself?

Do *two or more* of the following:

a) Help care for your clothes and be able to pack a suitcase. (See page 135.)

b) Make your bed and keep your room tidy for at least a week. (See page 136.)

c) Keep a piece of furniture clean for four weeks.

d) Make tea or coffee and serve it nicely. (See page 137.)

e) Make a salad or snack.

OR Help at home in some other way. (As you can see Emily and her Six have lots of ideas.)

Each time you help, colour in a brick on Freda's Memory Wall.

Ways of Helping

SCRUB A SAUCEPAN

DUST A ROOM

PEEL POTATOES FOR DINNER

VACUUM A CARPET

WASH THE SKIRTING BOARD

TIDY A CUPBOARD

CLEAN A WASH BASIN

EMPTY THE PEDAL BIN

HANG CLOTHES OUT TO DRY

POLISH A MIRROR

Put a tick beside the things which you have done.

Brownies Have Fun Out-of-Doors

The more you put into a Challenge, the more you get out of it.

Choose and do *one* of the following:

a) Follow a trail which has been laid in wool, string or some other material.

b) Grow a plant from a seed or a bulb. (See page 138.)

c) Care for a pet and over a period of time keep a record of what you do for it.

d) Make at least two types of rubbings (e.g. leaf rubbings, bark rubbings, floor or wall tile rubbings) and use them in an interesting way. (See page 139.)

OR Think up an Out-of-Doors Challenge of your own. (It may be linked to an Out-of-Doors Venture.)

Answer these questions when you have completed your Challenge.

What did you do? _____

How long did it take? _____

What did you enjoy about it? _____

_____

_____

At the end of your second Brownie Journey, just as at the end of your first, it is a good idea to think about your Promise.

Have you discovered any new ways of keeping it through the Challenges and Ventures you have done, and the Interest Badges you have gained?

DUTY TO GOD?
SERVING THE QUEEN?
HELPING OTHER PEOPLE?

CONGRATULATIONS

Try to spend a few moments chatting to your Guider about this. Perhaps she will be able to see your progress even more clearly than you can.

You are ready now to replace your Footpath Badge with the Brownie Road Badge.

'Guess what? When Linda, Karen and Helen moved up to Guides, Mrs James asked *me* to become Sixer of the Gnomes. So now I have a whole new Six to look after.'

'Perhaps you're wondering why we have so much luggage with us. It's because we're about to set off on the most exciting Brownie Venture of all . . . . . '

. . . Pack Holiday

'A Pack Holiday is a holiday Brownies spend together with their Pack; sleeping together, eating together, working together and playing together.

'For our Pack Holiday, we went to a big Brownie House near the sea. Every day different Sixes helped with the chores – cleaning, cooking and washing-up – so we were able to practise lots of skills we'd learnt on our Journeys, and to tackle new Challenges as well.

'We played games, went on expeditions and did all sorts of other things. What I enjoyed most was the story last thing at night, and Jill loved the pyjama party!'

'By the way, Brownies on Pack Holiday don't usually go around in their pyjamas. Proper Pack Holiday uniform is either a special brown short-sleeved dress, without a tie, or brown shorts or trousers with a yellow t-shirt.'

The Brownie Highway

Here is a map of the Brownie Journey you make when you are nine.

By the time you have completed these Challenges you will be a thoroughly experienced Brownie, ready to move on from the Brownie Highway to Guides.

TO THE GUIDES

HOSPITAL

BROWNIES LEND A HAND

BROWNIES KEEP FIT

BROWNIES ARE FRIENDLY

SPORTS CENTRE

AIRPORT

BROWNIES DO THEIR BEST

CONCERT HALL

PLACE OF WORSHIP

BROWNIES MAKE THINGS

TOWN HALL

BROWNIES HAVE FUN OUT OF DOORS

PARK

BROWNIES ARE WIDE AWAKE

HOME

BROWNIES HELP AT HOME

My Progress Along the Brownie Highway

Interest badges

Each time you complete a Challenge write the name on a section of the Highway.

When you take part in a Pack Venture write about it on a concrete slab in the Venture Bridge.

Write down any Interest Badges you gain on the right.

Brownies are Wide Awake ▬▬

There are many interesting and important things for Brownies to learn about their country.

Do at least *one* of the following:

a) Learn the first and last verses of the National Anthem, as written on page 99.

b) Learn how the Union Flag is made up. Know the country emblems and the stories of the Saints. (See page 140.)

c) Learn the Country Code and the reason for each part.

d) Find out about the story of your town's coat-of-arms. (See page 142.)

e) Describe an interesting place near your home.

OR Learn something else of interest or importance about where you live.

Colour in this Union Flag when you have completed your Challenges.

The Country Code

1. Enjoy the countryside and respect its life and work.

2. Guard against all risk of fire.

3. Fasten all gates.

4. Keep your dogs under close control.

5. Keep to public paths across farmland.

6. Use gates and stiles to cross fences, hedges and walls.

7. Leave livestock, crops and machinery alone.

8. Take your litter home.

9. Help to keep all water clean.

10. Protect wildlife, plants and trees.

11. Take special care on country roads.

12. Make no unnecessary noise.

Many people know the first verse of the National Anthem, but the last verse is less familiar. Here are the words of both verses.

The National Anthem

God save our gracious Queen,
Long live our noble Queen,
God save the Queen!
Send her victorious,
Happy and Glorious,
Long to reign over us,
God save the Queen!

Thy choicest gifts in store
On her be pleased to pour,
Long may she reign.
May she defend our laws,
And ever give us cause
To sing with heart and voice,
God save the Queen!

Brownies Keep Healthy

On the Brownie Road you found out that certain foods do not keep you fit and healthy. There are other things which can actually damage your health. People who smoke or drink too much alcohol run serious risks of disease, and the risks are even greater for those who become addicted to drugs or solvents (such as glue).

In a group or on your own, make a poster warning against the harm these things can do. Look at page 59 on the Footpath where you labelled different parts of the body. Discuss with your Guider the parts which are harmed by the abuse of tobacco, alcohol, solvents and drugs.

Do *one* of the following:

a) Walk a figure of eight balancing a ball on a book. Try using the hand you don't write with.

b) Make up a sequence of three or four different skipping steps.

c) With a bat, hit a ball that has been bowled to you, four times out of five.

d) Show that you have made progress in a sport which interests you, e.g. swimming, skating or riding.

OR Challenge yourself in some other form of exercise.

Put a tick in the box opposite the Challenge you have chosen.

100

I KEEP HEALTHY BY TAKING CARE OF MY APPEARANCE!

Do you look your best?

How many boxes can you tick in a week?

I WASHED MY FACE MORNING AND NIGHT

I CLEANED MY TEETH AFTER MEALS

I BRUSHED MY HAIR AT LEAST TWICE A DAY

I HAD AT LEAST 8 HOURS SLEEP

I ATE SOME FRESH FRUIT OR SALAD

Brownies Do their Best

Often other people can't tell if you are keeping the first part of your Promise, but on the Highway you are challenged to keep it in a way that can be seen.

For a period of time (more than one week) carry out *one* of the following:

a) Help in your place of worship in some special way, e.g. cleaning.

b) Make up, write down and illustrate prayers for the Pack or Pack Prayer Book.

c) Make up and illustrate a Thank You God Chart.

d) With the Pack, take part in a Good Turn Venture.

OR Think about the first part of your Promise and Do Your Best in some other way.

| I DO MY BEST |

Write about your Challenge here:

Sophie Mum Dad

nipper

my school

buses

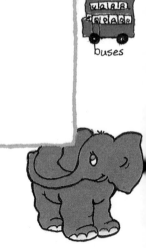

Round the edge Emily has drawn pictures of things she wants to thank God for. Why not make some Thank You pictures of your own.

Brownies Make Things

On the Footpath and the Road most of your Challenges involved making something with your hands. On the Highway, you have the opportunity to use your voice, arms, legs and memory as well.

Do *one or more* of the following:

a) Take part in an entertainment by singing, acting, miming, dancing, reciting, playing an instrument or working a puppet, either alone or with others. (See page 144.)

b) With your family, school or Brownie Pack, take part in a theatre visit. Write or talk about it at a Pack Meeting.

c) Make up a story, poem or short play and use it to give pleasure to someone.

d) Make an article for a gift.

e) Try a craft new to you, e.g. weaving, embroidery or papier-mâché. (See page 143.)

OR Challenge yourself to be creative (i.e. to make something) in some other way.

The younger members of Emily's Six made puppets when they were on the Footpath. When Emily was on the Highway, she wrote a short play. They put their heads together and here they are entertaining the whole Pack!

Answer these questions when you have
completed your Challenge:

What did you do?

_____

_____

What was the most difficult part?

_____

_____

Were you happy with the way it turned
out?

_____

_____

Can you say why?

_____

_____

There are a lot of Interest Badges connected
with this Challenge. If you gain any, draw
them below.

Brownies are Friendly

The Brownie Highway may not transport you to another country, but it does give you an opportunity to learn more about your Guide and Brownie friends around the world.

Do *one* of the following:

a) Find out about the World Badge and, on a map point out ten countries where there are Brownies.

b) Make a scrap book about another country where there are Brownies. (See page 145.)

c) Find out how Guiding began and make a display about it to show to your Six.

OR Challenge yourself in some other way to learn more about Brownies abroad.

Write down some things you discovered when doing this Challenge.

_____

_____

_____

_____

_____

_____

_____

_____

Brownies Lend a Hand

One of the places you visit on the Highway
is the hospital. A Brownie who knows how
to deal with a minor accident, or who can
prevent one happening in the first place,
can lend doctors and nurses a hand.

Remember to do a Good Turn every day
and do *one* of the following:

a) Learn how to prevent simple cuts, grazes
and nose bleeds from becoming worse.
(See page 146.)

b) Learn how to deal with clothes on fire
and how to treat simple burns.
(See page 148.)

c) When out in the area where you live,
make a list of the hazards you can find.

OR Lend a Hand to prevent accidents or
give first aid in some other way.

Colour in the letters when you have
completed your Challenge, and write what
you did underneath.

A GOOD TURN
A DAY
KEEPS BOREDOM
AWAY!

Did you spot any of these hazards in your area? What sort of accidents could they cause?

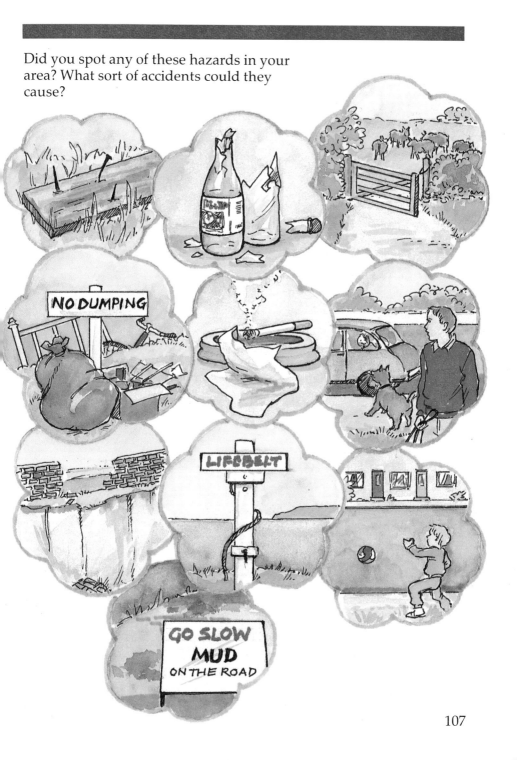

Brownies Help at Home

A Brownie on the Highway is asked to tackle some really skilful jobs around the house.

Do *two or more* of the following:

a) Make scones or cakes or make something useful from a recipe. (See page 149.)

b) Defrost OR clean out the refrigerator.

c) Help an adult to clean a car.

d) Learn to repair clothes and sew on a button or badge. (See page 150-51.)

e) Learn to iron a simple garment safely and learn the meanings of the symbols on clothes labels.

OR Help at Home in some other way.

I Help at Home

For my Challenge I _____

_____

_____

Which two Interest Badges will help you to learn more about this Challenge?

Draw and colour them in if you gain them.

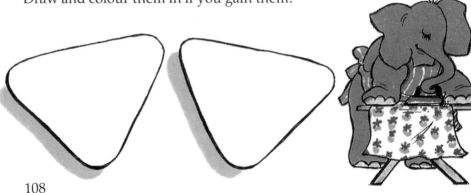

Brownies Have Fun Out-of-Doors

Getting lost is no fun! Neither is missing a bus, nor looking out on a garden full of weeds!

Choose and do *one* of the following:

a) Set a compass and know eight of its points. (See page 152.)

b) Make a simple map showing the area surrounding your Pack Meeting place or your home. Give directions that would be useful to a stranger, e.g. to the nearest shop, the nearest telephone or to the hospital.

c) Send a secret message to someone who is out of hearing range, using signals or codes. (See page 153.)

d) Read a bus or train timetable and know the 24-hour clock.

e) With your parents' permission, take care of a garden, window box or tub.

OR Do something else that will help you to Have Fun Out-of-Doors.

Record what you did for this Challenge in the space below.

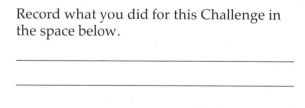

Do you think that what you have just learnt will be useful when you leave Brownies for Guides? Can you say why?

Now is the time to find out as much as you can about the things Guides do.

One Journey Ends . . .

Like you, Emily has completed her eight Highway Challenges and has reached the end of her third Brownie Journey. Last week she replaced her Brownie Road Badge with the Brownie Highway Badge.

'I've learnt so much in my three years as a Brownie,' she told Mrs James. 'Especially about my Promise. It really makes a difference to everything I do – not just at Brownie meetings, but at home and even at school.'

Can you understand what she meant? What sort of difference does your Promise make at home and at school? Perhaps you could discuss this with your Guider, and then, at the back of your Handbook, try to note down some important things you have learnt over the last three years.

THERE'S A SPECIAL PART FOR ME IN VENTURES!

I HAVE FRIENDS ALL OVER THE WORLD

I ENJOY A REAL CHALLENGE!

IT'S FUN TO LAH!

. . . And Another Begins

Has your Guider given you a copy of the *Brownie Trefoil Book* yet?

This little book is specially designed to prepare you for a very special journey – from Brownies into Guides.

When Emily was given her *Brownie Trefoil Book* she went straight round to Linda's house.

THERE ARE SO MANY THINGS I WANT TO KNOW ABOUT GUIDES. CAN YOU HELP ME?

One by one Emily's questions were answered. The Guide Promise is almost the same as the Brownie Promise, she discovered, and Guides have Laws and a Motto just like Brownies. They have fun too, in their small groups (called Patrols not Sixes). They work for badges (rather like Brownie Interest and Journey Badges, but more adventurous), and go on expeditions together, cooking meals outside and sometimes camping.

LET'S GO UP TO MY ROOM.

COOKING OUTSIDE! **WOW!** WILL I DO THAT?

OF COURSE! NOW YOU'RE TEN YOU'RE READY TO BE ONE OF US AND JOIN IN ALL OUR ACTIVITIES.

111

Perhaps you don't have an older friend like Linda to explain about Guides, but there are other ways of getting information.

★ You could ask your Pack Leader.

Pack Leaders know all about Guides. Your Pack Leader will be able to tell you where the Company meets and when, what the Patrols are called, the names of the Guiders and all sorts of other interesting things.

★ You could read *Today's Guide*.

Guides, like Brownies, have their own magazine. Your Guider will probably be able to get you a copy.

★ You could visit the Company.

No matter how well someone describes a Guide meeting, nothing beats being at one for yourself. Your Guider will arrange this for you, but it's up to you to make the most of the opportunity and find out as much as you can.

COME AND MEET OUR GUIDES.

DON'T FORGET TO SAY **THANK YOU !**

Before you go to Guides see how many of the following you can tick:

I visited a Guide Camp-fire. ☐

I completed my *Brownie Trefoil Book*. ☐

I know how Guides began. ☐

I have taken part in a Friendship Venture. ☐

I found an idea in *The Brownie* and have made something. ☐

I have talked to a friend on a telephone made from tin-cans and string. ☐

I have met my Patrol Leader. ☐

I have ordered *Today's Guide* from the newsagent. ☐

The Brownie Trefoil Badge ▬

This is the badge you will take with you
from Brownies to Guides.

The Brownie Trefoil Badge is worn on the
left shoulder of your new uniform. Not
only does it show other people you've been
a Brownie, but it also reminds you of the
fun you've had and the things you've
learnt on Ventures and Journeys (things
that will be very useful to you as a Guide).

According to Emily, there's even
MORE fun ahead.

GUIDES ARE
FANTASTIC!

SEE YOU THERE!

How To . . . .

Hints on the Brownie Footpath

How to throw a bean bag.

1 Aim for the centre of your target.

2 Hold the bean bag lightly in the tips of your fingers.

3 Look at your target as you throw.

4 For a strong throw, stand with one shoulder and foot forward and use your whole body.

How to skip backwards

1 Make sure your rope is the right length. (When you stand with your arms out straight, it should touch your toes.)

2 Stand straight, making a T shape with your arms; swing the rope backwards and jump just high enough for it to pass beneath your feet.

3 A slight bounce as the rope passes over your head will help you to time your jumps correctly.

How to bounce a ball without a break.

1 Keep your eye on the ball.

2 Don't bounce it too hard.

3 Practise and your score will increase.

How to jump the Blob

The blob is a bean bag fastened to a rope about three metres long. One Brownie swings the bag in a circle while her friend jumps over the rope.

You will need to be wide awake for this Challenge!

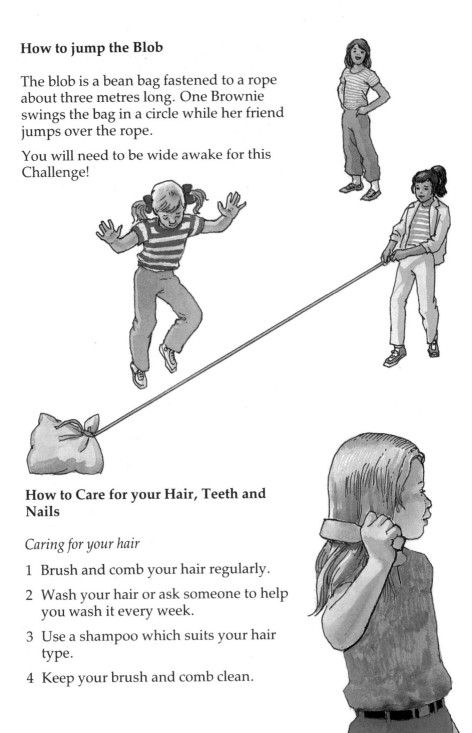

How to Care for your Hair, Teeth and Nails

Caring for your hair

1 Brush and comb your hair regularly.

2 Wash your hair or ask someone to help you wash it every week.

3 Use a shampoo which suits your hair type.

4 Keep your brush and comb clean.

Caring for your teeth

1 Always brush your teeth before going to bed and after meals if possible.

2 Use toothpaste and a small head toothbrush with medium bristles.

3 Brush up and down as well as from side to side. Rinse your mouth thoroughly with water.

4 Try not to eat too many sugary sweets. They are bad for your teeth.

Caring for your nails

1 Keep your nails fairly short, using nail scissors or an emery board.

2 Clean your nails regularly.

3 Milk contains calcium, which helps to make nails strong. Strengthen your nails by drinking some every day.

4 If you bite your nails, care for them by giving them the chance to grow. This is a REAL Challenge!

Some general hints:

1 Check that you have all the things you will need before you begin.

2 If you are going to use glue, paint or spray, cover the table with newspaper.

3 Sometimes you will need to set your work to one side for a while. Make sure it is in a safe place, and that it isn't in anyone's way.

4 Remember to tidy up when you have finished.

How to make a snowman decoration

You will need:

A cream or yoghurt carton
A ball of crumpled paper
Cotton wool
A strip of coloured felt
A circle of black felt

2 currants
A small piece of glacé cherry
3 jelly tots or other sweets
A liquorice all-sort (or other suitable sweet)
glue

1 Make the snowman's body by gluing the ball of paper onto the narrow end of the carton. Cover both with cotton wool.

2 Make the mouth, eyes and buttons by gluing the cherry, currants and jelly tots into place.

3 Glue the liquorice all-sort onto the circle of felt to make a hat.

4 Stick the hat to the snowman's head and finish by tying the strip of felt around his neck to make a scarf.

120

How to make a glove puppet

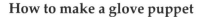

You will need:

A matchbox
Some plain paper and felt tip pens
A piece of furry material or some wool
A piece of material twice the size of your hand
Scissors, needle and thread

1 Cover the matchbox with plain paper and draw a face on it.

2 Make the hair by sticking on a piece of furry material or some wool.

3 Make a hole for your finger in the box.

4 Place your hand on a sheet of paper, tucking away your last two fingers. Draw round your hand to make a pattern.

5 Cut two pieces of cloth to this shape and sew them together.

6 With your hand in the glove and the matchbox in position, you are ready to entertain your friends.

N.B. Matchboxes are useful for making all sorts of things, so it is a good idea to collect them.

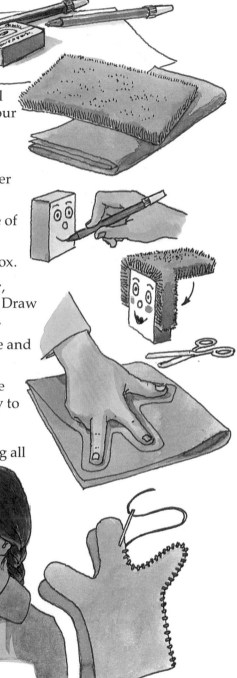

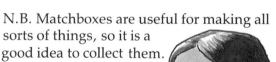

121

How to make some Pack equipment

Here are some pieces of equipment you could make:

a ball out of newspaper and a pair of old tights.

a bean bag out of cloth and dried peas, beans or some other filling.

skittles out of empty plastic bottles washed inside, scrubbed outside and filled with sand or dried peas.

a musical instrument; maracas, for example, from plastic containers filled with rice or gravel.

stilts out of tin cans threaded with string.

Try to choose something your Pack really needs (not another bean bag if there's already a boxful in the cupboard) and take time to decorate your work. The equipment you make should be useful and should look nice.

How to lay a table

Here is a place set for a special meal.

The knife is on the right and the fork is on the left. The small knife is placed outside the larger knife, and the dessert spoon belongs above the place-mat, with the dessert fork underneath.

Look at the picture carefully. What else can you see? There's a cup and saucer on the right, a side-plate on the left and on top of the side-plate there's a serviette.

Now try to remember where everything goes and practise setting a place without looking at the book.

What else might you need on the table besides cutlery and crockery?

How to clean muddy shoes

1 Cover the surface you are working on with newspaper and protect your clothes with an apron.

2 Remove the mud from the shoes. (It will come off easily if you allow it to dry.)

3 Choose a polish that matches the colour of the shoes.

4 Look at the shoe brushes. Usually there are two sorts – brushes for polishing and brushes for shining. You will know which is which because a shining brush is much cleaner than a polishing brush.

5 Using the polishing brush, carefully cover the toes, heels and sides of the shoes with polish.

6 Now use the shining brush (or wrap the polishing brush in a duster or rag) rubbing it over the shoes, backwards and forwards, up and down until they gleam.

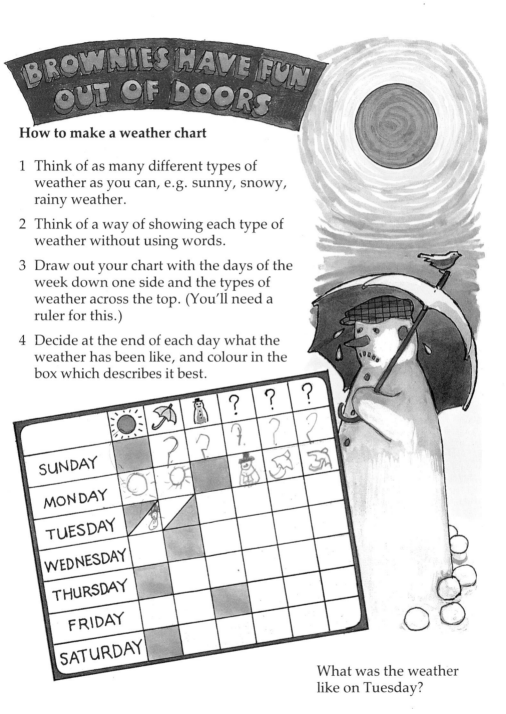

BROWNIES HAVE FUN OUT OF DOORS

How to make a weather chart

1 Think of as many different types of weather as you can, e.g. sunny, snowy, rainy weather.

2 Think of a way of showing each type of weather without using words.

3 Draw out your chart with the days of the week down one side and the types of weather across the top. (You'll need a ruler for this.)

4 Decide at the end of each day what the weather has been like, and colour in the box which describes it best.

	☀	☂	☃	?	?	?
SUNDAY						
MONDAY						
TUESDAY						
WEDNESDAY						
THURSDAY						
FRIDAY						
SATURDAY						

What was the weather like on Tuesday?

BROWNIES ARE WIDE AWAKE

How to make a call from a public telephone box.

Making a telephone call from a phone-box is not difficult, but you do need to recognise the kind of telephone you are using. Today there are three main types: old style coin boxes, newer push-button coin boxes and card phones. Here are instructions for using each kind:

Old-style coin phones

1 Lift the receiver and dial the number you require.

2 You should hear a ringing sound which will change to a quick 'pip . . . pip . . . ', when the phone is answered.

3 As soon as you hear this, insert your money in the coin slot. (These phones only accept 10p coins.)

4 The pips will stop and you can speak.

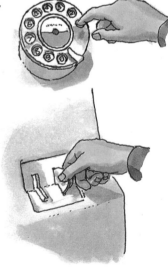

Push-button coin phones

1 Unhook the receiver and insert your money. Sometimes you can use coins of different values in these phones, and the amount you have inserted will be displayed in a small box above the buttons.)

2 Push the buttons to obtain the number you require.

3 Watch the figures in the box during your call and you will see how much money is being used. When there is none left your call is cut off so have some money ready in case you need it.

4 When you have finished, replace the receiver and any unused coins will be returned to you. (Remember the machine cannot give change, so if you are making a short call use smaller value coins.)

Card phones

Card phones only work when a special phonecard is inserted. For your call however, the best plan is probably to use the nearest coin phone.

Some general hints

Always dial the number carefully, remembering to include the correct code if you are phoning outside your own area.

Emergency Calls

In an emergency dial 999. You won't need any money for this. The operator will ask whether you require Police, the Fire Brigade or the Ambulance. Answer clearly and calmly and help will soon be on its way. Don't forget to give the address.

How to mind your tongue

1 Remember the words please and thank you, and use them as often as you can.

2 When you are angry, count to ten before you speak.

3 Fine yourself one penny every time you grumble at meal-times. Give the money to help those who do not have enough to eat.

4 It takes two to make a quarrel. See how many quarrels you can stop.

5 When you do something wrong, don't let your tongue make excuses. Make it say sorry.

128

How to make a gift using natural materials.

Here are some ideas you might like to try. First look at the pictures and see if you can work out what materials they've been made with. The answers are given underneath.

A paperweight

A smooth stone, cleaned, painted and varnished.

An ornament

The tortoise is made from six seashells glued together.

A necklace

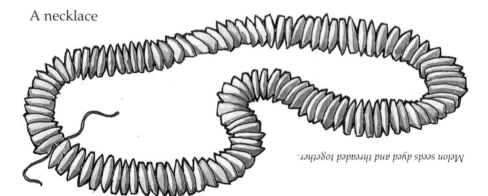

Melon seeds dyed and threaded together.

BROWNIES MAKE THINGS

How to sew, knit and crochet

The best way of learning any of these is to find someone to show you.

Begin by making something very simple and don't be afraid to ask for help.

If you are interested in sewing here are some suggestions to try.

Oven-gloves

A traycloth or cushion cover

A bean-bag

A purse

A pencil-case

An apron

When sewing remember the following rules:

1 Start your work firmly either with a knot (which you then hide) or by going over your first stitch twice.

2 Never leave a raw edge. Always turn a hem.

3 Use pins and big stitches (called tacking) to hold the material in position before sewing it properly.

4 Join the sides of a purse or a pencil case together by oversewing.

5 Neat, evenly-spaced stitches in a colourful thread can be part of the pattern of your work.

6 Finish your work off well. You don't want it coming apart at the seams!

Knitting

Perhaps you are more interested in knitting than sewing. On the next page you will find diagrams showing how to knit garter stitch. Once you have learned this stitch, you can knit many things – not only blankets and scarves, but all sorts of toys as well. (Your Guider will know where the patterns for these can be found.)

Garter stitch is easy. All you have to do is
remember four words:

IN

Push needle B into the stitch.

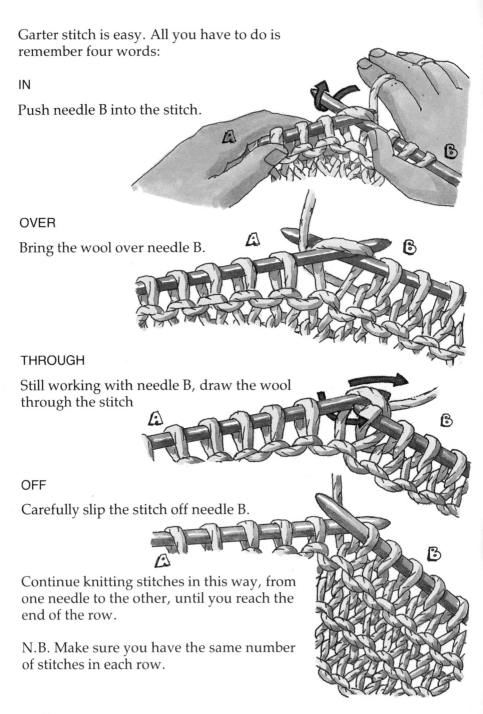

OVER

Bring the wool over needle B.

THROUGH

Still working with needle B, draw the wool
through the stitch

OFF

Carefully slip the stitch off needle B.

Continue knitting stitches in this way, from
one needle to the other, until you reach the
end of the row.

N.B. Make sure you have the same number
of stitches in each row.

Crochet

As a change from sewing and knitting you might like to try crochet. Crochet grows very quickly, and it is also very easy to unravel if you go wrong.

The first crochet stitch you will learn is called chain stitch, and looks like this:

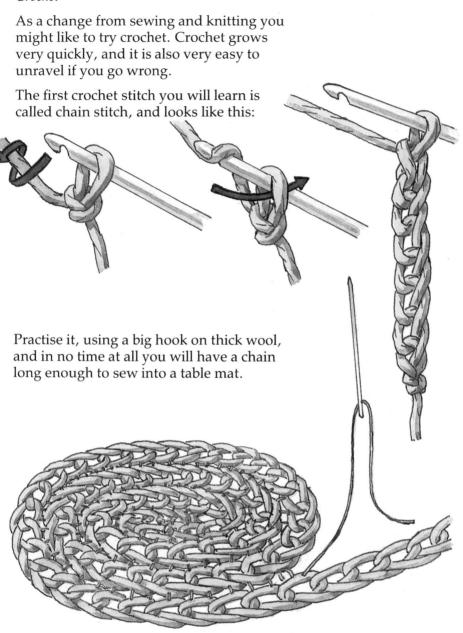

Practise it, using a big hook on thick wool, and in no time at all you will have a chain long enough to sew into a table mat.

How to keep your home safe

Many accidents in the home are caused by carelessness. The more careful you are, the safer your home will be.

Here are some examples of carelessness:

1 A fire without a guard.

2 A television set or toaster left plugged in overnight.

3 Saucepans on the cooker with the handles facing outwards.

4 An open drawer with a knife blade sticking out.

5 Front and back doors left unlocked at night.

6 A plastic bag in the same room as a small child.

7 A bottle of coloured tablets left on the table.

8 A box of matches on the carpet beside the fire.

9 A mirror hanging above the fireplace.

10 Bleach in a cup beside the sink.

11 Cooking oil spilt on the floor and not properly cleared up.

12 A wrinkled carpet at the top of the stairs.

What could happen as a result? (You will find more information about keeping your home safe in the booklet on the Safety in the Home Badge.)

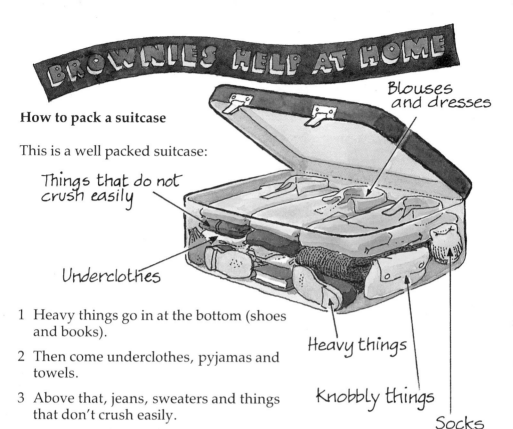

BROWNIES HELP AT HOME

Blouses
and dresses

How to pack a suitcase

This is a well packed suitcase:

Things that do not
crush easily

Underclothes

1 Heavy things go in at the bottom (shoes and books).

2 Then come underclothes, pyjamas and towels.

3 Above that, jeans, sweaters and things that don't crush easily.

4 At the very top are skirts and t-shirts.

5 Knobbly things such as your wash-bag fit in at the sides.

6 Socks can be squeezed into the corners.

Heavy things

Knobbly things

Socks

As you can see, the clothes have been folded into rectangles. This means they fit neatly into the case.

Before beginning to pack, it is a good idea to make a list of the things you will need. (You don't want to end up like a Brownie who had to miss her first pyjama party because she'd forgotten her pyjamas.)

135

How to make a bed

An unmade bed means an untidy room!

To make your bed properly:

1 Begin by stripping it completely.

2 Replace the bottom sheet tucking the wide hem in at the top. Smooth to remove wrinkles, then tuck the sides in neatly.

3 Shake your pillow and put it back in position.

4 Replace the top sheet with about 30cm to spare at the top for turning down over the blankets.

5 Replace the blankets tucking them in one by one.

6 Turn down the top sheet.

7 Finally replace the bedspread.

You may have a duvet instead of blankets on your bed. This makes bed-making easier, but you will still need to straighten the bottom sheet and arrange your quilt so it lies smoothly.

How to make tea

1 Fill the kettle with fresh water from the tap. Boil it.

2 Warm the tea-pot with a little boiled water.

3 To make tea for four people, put three teaspoons of tea or two teabags into the pot. (For two people use two teaspoons of tea or one teabag.)

4 Take the tea-pot to the kettle and pour boiling water onto the tea.

5 Let the tea stand for 3–5 minutes before pouring it.

6 If you are using tea-leaves instead of teabags use a tea-strainer as you pour the tea.

How to make coffee for a visitor

1 Put one teaspoon of instant coffee per person into a warmed coffee-pot or jug.

2 Pour on boiling water – about one mugful for each person.

3 Stir well.

4 Serve immediately with warm or cold milk.

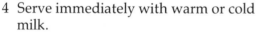

How to grow a hyacinth bulb

1 Put a few pebbles into the bottom of a bowl for drainage. Thoroughly wet some bulb fibre in a bucket, squeeze it well and then half fill the bowl. (You may use compost instead of bulb fibre if you prefer.)

2 Place the bulb in the bowl, but do not force it into the fibre. Fill the bowl with more fibre until only the tip of the bulb can be seen.

3 Leave the bulb in a dark airy place (some people use a black polythene bag with holes to let the air in) and keep the fibre damp.

4 When the shoot is about 3cm long, move the bowl into a shady spot in a cool room. The leaves will now develop and within a few weeks the flower buds will appear.

5 Move the bulb to a lighter spot for flowering. (You can plant the bulb in the garden after it has flowered).

How to make a bark rubbing

Have you ever looked closely at the bark of a tree? Or compared the bark of an Oak with the bark of a Chestnut? Making a bark rubbing is one way in which you can really learn to appreciate the different patterns.

1 Tape a strong piece of drawing paper to the trunk of the tree.

2 Rub a piece of chalk or wax crayon across the surface of the paper until it is completely covered.

3 You should now be able to see the pattern of the bark clearly.

4 Write the name of the tree on the back of the rubbing. Try also to note its height and the width of the trunk.

5 Store your rubbings in a folder between sheets of card.

Leaf rubbings and floor or wall-tile rubbings can be made in much the same way, using finer paper and charcoal, or a soft lead pencil.

Hints on the Brownie Highway

BROWNIES ARE WIDE AWAKE

How the Union Flag is made up

This is the Union Flag, the flag you will see flying in England, Scotland, Northern Ireland and Wales. It is made up using crosses in a special way to show that these countries together form the United Kingdom. (A union means a joining together.)

In the background is the cross of St. Andrew, the patron saint of Scotland.

Then comes the cross of St. Patrick, the patron saint of Ireland.

Finally we have the cross of St. George, the patron saint of England.

The patron saint of Wales is St. David, and the Welsh national flag looks like this.

There are four days each year when we particularly remember these saints.

On 17th March, we remember St. Patrick. As a boy he was kidnapped and taken to Ireland as a slave. He escaped, but later returned to spend the rest of his life telling Irish people about God.

On 23rd April, we remember St. George. Folk tales tell us that he was a soldier who always tried to obey God. He once saved a princess very bravely, and was always ready to help other people.

On 30th November, we remember St. Andrew. He was a fisherman and a special friend of Jesus.

On 1st March, we remember St. David. Wherever he went, he comforted and helped people. Sometimes he did this by singing to them, for he had a most wonderful voice.

The stories of the saints are interesting to read. Perhaps you can borrow a book about them from your Guider or from your local library.

How to find out about your town's coat-of-arms

The earliest coats-of-arms were real coats, worn by knights over their armour. Each coat was embroidered with a special coloured pattern which matched the pattern on the knight's shield. In battle these patterns helped show the difference between the knight's friends and enemies.

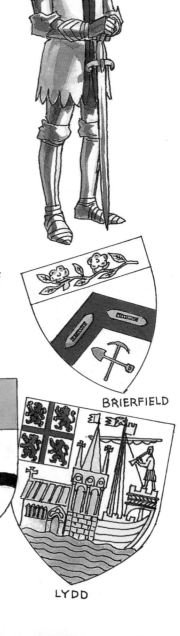

Today a coat-of-arms is not something you wear. It is a kind of badge with a special pattern, which tells the history of the person or place to which it belongs.

The coat-of-arms of an industrial town, for example, may show tools such as a weaver's shuttle.

The best place to find out about your town's coat-of-arms is at the public library. Ask the librarian for some information or a book on the subject. You could also make a sketch and colour it – it could be the start of a very interesting collection.

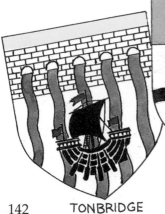

BRIERFIELD

TONBRIDGE

BLACKBURN

LYDD

BROWNIES MAKE THINGS

How to make a papier-mâché flower-pot

Papier-mâché is what the name sounds like – a mash of paper. A flower-pot like this for dried or artificial flowers is very easy to make.

All you need is newspaper, flour, water, an old flower-pot and some gloss paint.

1 Tear the newspaper into small pieces and soak them in water overnight.

2 When they are soft and pulpy, drain off the water.

3 Add enough flour to make a dough.

4 Turn the flower-pot upside down and spread the mash over the outside of the pot.

5 Make a pattern by pressing your fingers and thumbs into the papier-mâché.

6 Leave the pot to dry thoroughly.

7 When dry, paint it with gloss paint inside and out.

How to put on an entertainment for the rest of the Pack

Brownies usually enjoy acting, but sometimes find it hard to learn lines. You can solve this problem by getting the best reader in your Six to read a story or poem while the rest of the Six mime the actions.

Some stories you could mime are: *The Brownie Story, Cinderella* or *Jack and the Beanstalk*, a fable such as *The Hare and the Tortoise*, or your own story (remember it needs to be short and to have plenty of action).

Some poems you could mime are: *The Owl and The Pussy Cat* by Edward Lear, *The Pied Piper of Hamlin* by Robert Browning, *Father William* by Lewis Caroll. Perhaps your Guider could suggest other suitable poems.

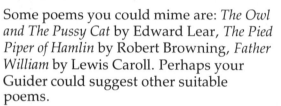

How to make a scrapbook about another country where there are Brownies

1 First you must find out as much as you can about the country you have chosen (size, population, climate, language, food, name of the capital city, national costume etc.) Do you know anyone who has lived there? Why not ask them for help? Your local tourist office may be worth a visit and you can gain a lot of information from geography books and encyclopaedias.

2 As well as information you will need illustrations for your scrapbook. Try to collect maps, pictures of people in national costume, brochures, postcards, stamps and money (coins or notes). Keep these things in a large envelope until you are ready to use them.

3 Plan your scrapbook carefully, deciding what to put on each page.

4 Begin work, one page at a time. Make each page as interesting and as colourful as you can. (Copy headings and bits of information onto plain paper rather than writing directly onto the page.)

5 Be careful with the glue. If you use too much, you will end up with sticky smudges round the edges!

6 Cover your completed scrapbook with sticky plastic or stiff paper. Make a title for the front cover and write your name inside.

145

How to prevent simple cuts and grazes from becoming worse

The most important thing is to keep the wound clean.

1 Clean your hands by washing them.

2 Clean the wound using water and a clean rag or cotton wool.

3 Keep the wound clean by covering it with an adhesive dressing such as elastoplast or a piece of gauze held in position with bandage. (You will find out how to tie and bandage in one of the badge booklets.)

How to treat a nose bleed

1 Tell the patient to sit with her head tipped slightly forward.

2 Firmly pinch the soft part of her nose.

3 Do not let the patient blow her nose.

4 Tell an adult what has happened.

146

How to deal with clothes on fire

1 Wrap a coat or rug around the person, calling for help at the same time.

2 Push her to the ground.

3 Roll her over and beat out the flames.

4 Make her comfortable.

5 Fetch an adult immediately.

If you don't have anything to wrap around the burning clothes, make the patient stand still, push her onto the ground and roll her over and over.

How to treat simple burns and scalds

1 Cool the affected area by placing it in cold water or under a gently running tap.

2 Keep in cold water until the pain eases.

3 Do not prick or break blisters.

4 Do not put lotions, antiseptics or anything greasy onto the burn.

5 Wash your hands thoroughly and cover the burn with a light, sterile dressing such as a clean cotton handkerchief. Do not use hairy or fluffy material.

How to make small cakes

Some general hints on baking:

1 Put on an apron and wash your hands before you begin.

2 Turn on the oven at the start, so that it will have reached the correct temperature by the time you are ready to use it.

3 Read the recipe carefully; make sure you have all the ingredients.

4 If you are using cake tins, grease them well, or your cakes might stick.

5 Measure your ingredients carefully using scales or a tablespoon.

   One rounded tablespoon of flour = 25gm (1oz)
   One level tablespoon of sugar = 25gm (1oz)

6 Keep an eye on the clock while your cakes are in the oven, but don't open the oven door too soon or they will go flat.

7 Always clear the table and wash up when you have finished.

Method:

Beat together the margarine and sugar in a bowl using a wooden spoon or an electric mixer until it looks a pale colour. Add the eggs a little at a time, beating well. Gently stir in the flour and salt with a tablespoon. Divide the mixture into paper cake cases or bun tins and bake for 15–20 minutes in a warm oven set at 190°C (175F) or Gas Mark 5.

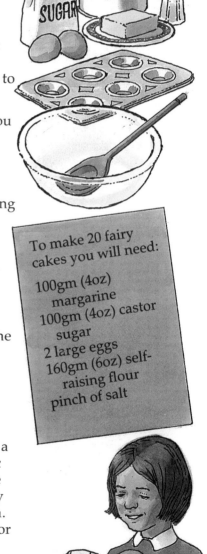

To make 20 fairy cakes you will need:

100gm (4oz) margarine
100gm (4oz) castor sugar
2 large eggs
160gm (6oz) self-raising flour
pinch of salt

How to sew on a button

1 Decide where you are going to put the button. Secure the thread to that spot either with a knot or by making a small stitch and going over it twice.

2 Slide the button down the thread.

3 Sew the button into position by working the needle down through one hole and up through another.

4 When the button is secure, wind the thread tightly several times around its base.

5 Finish off with a double stitch on the wrong side of the material.

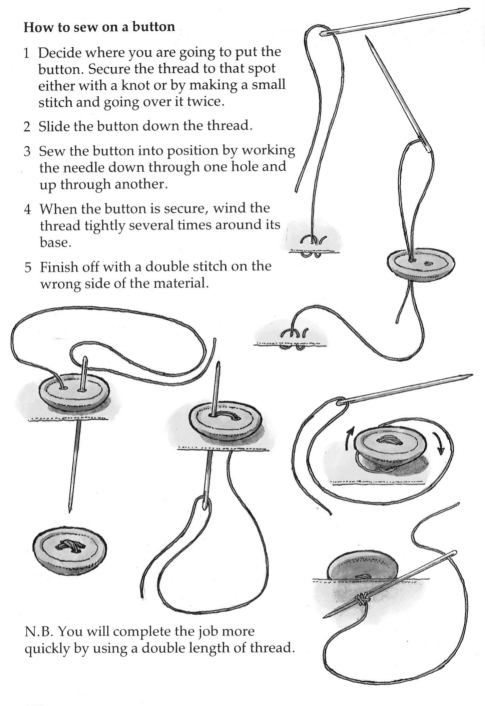

N.B. You will complete the job more quickly by using a double length of thread.

How to sew on a badge

1 Use dark thread – either black or brown.

2 Find the correct place to wear the badge and pin it into position.

3 Make three small stitches in the same place.

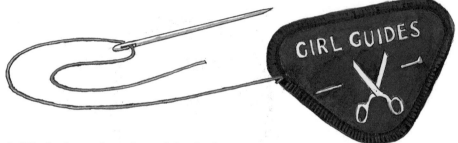

4 Work along the edge of the badge attaching it to your uniform with evenly spaced diagonal stitches. (This stitch may also be used to turn down a raw edge.)

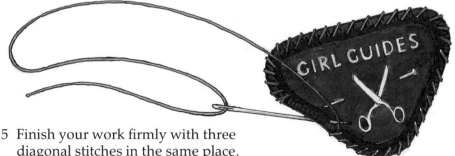

5 Finish your work firmly with three diagonal stitches in the same place.

How to set a compass

Imagine you are on a hiking expedition
deep in the country. To reach the nearest
village you must walk in a south-easterly
direction. How can you tell what direction
that is? If you happen to have a compass in
your rucksack, you can get your bearings
very easily.

1 Place the compass on a flat surface.

2 Wait until the needle settles and is
  pointing constantly in the same
  direction. That direction is North.

3 Carefully turn the rim of the compass
  (without disturbing the needle until the
  North marking points in the direction of
  the needle. The compass is now set.

4 It is now easy to work out where the
  south-east lies and you can continue
  your journey confidently.

How to signal a message using semaphore

This is the semaphore alphabet.

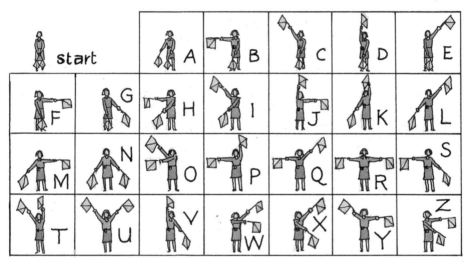

Some general hints:

1 The signalling may be done with flags or simply with your arms. (Semaphore may also be written.)

2 Keep your body straight and your feet slightly apart.

3 Never move from one letter until you're sure of the position of the next.

4 Bring your arms down in front of you at the end of each word.

5 Signal slowly and evenly.

6 If you make a mistake, signal E eight times.

Now see if you can decipher this message:

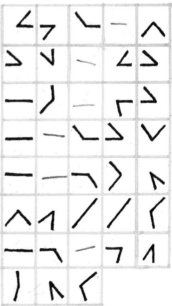

Index